The Book of Funny Signs

From Signs & Wonders in

Dalesman

First published in 2009 by Dalesman Publishing
an imprint of
Country Publications Ltd
The Water Mill, Broughton Hall
Skipton, North Yorkshire BD23 3AG

Reprinted 2010, 2011, 2013, 2014, 2016

ISBN 978-1-85568-267-2

Printed in China by 1010 Printing Ltd

Introduction

Have you ever thought that, in this modern world we live in, there are too many instructions, warnings, advertising boards and other signs and notices cluttering up our lives? Luckily, they are not all serious, and there are plenty that incite a chuckle, whether deliberately or not.

Over the years, *Dalesman* magazine has printed a selection of amusing and strange signs in its Signs & Wonders column, that our readers have spotted and laughed at while out and about in Yorkshire.

We are indebted to all *Dalesman* readers who have sent these in, and here we share a selection of the best ones for your enjoyment.

24

INVESTMENTS
PENSIONS
MORTGAGES
SCHOOL FEES
SAVINGS PLANS

SMITH & PINCHING

ANTIQUES

JOHN WILSON & SON
FUNERAL DIRECTORS
TEL. 01423 322508/324642

RESTORATION
SERVICE

74

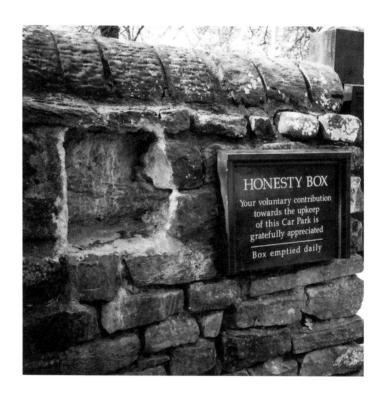

Pedestrian & Cyclist Recycling Area

→

Crecycle for York

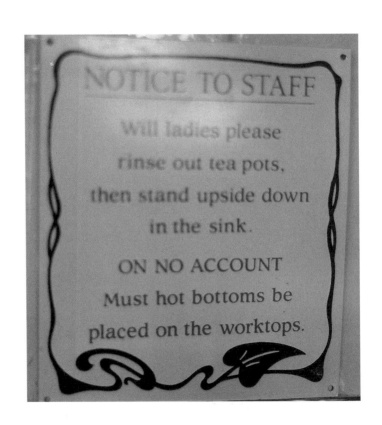

NOTICE TO STAFF

Will ladies please
rinse out tea pots,
then stand upside down
in the sink.

ON NO ACCOUNT
Must hot bottoms be
placed on the worktops.

WHEEL CLAMPING
IN OPERATION
FIXED PENALTY £100

ENJOY YOUR STAY

Acknowledgements

Thanks to the following *Dalesman* readers for their photographs:

Denis Aston
Ken Benson
Mrs W Billups
Peter Blakeney
Alan Booth
Steve Braddock
Miss T Bradley
J Brewer
Chris Broadribb
Betty de Brouwer
Jon Brownridge
Geoff Butterfield
Mrs Marie Caltieri
Colin Calvert
Dick Clark
Mr A M Clay
Mr R E Coates
Ray Corcoran
Mike Cowen
George Crompton
Ruth and Freddie Daniel
Maurice Dobson
Mr and Mrs R Drawater
Mrs Anne Ellerington
Miss Marjorie Emsley
Sam and Lynne Featherstone
Tom Fothergill
Mr F Fox
Hector Fraser

Mrs M L Frear
Ron Gibson
Joe Graham
John and Marion Green
Edmund Gregory
Joe Hakeney
John Halhead
Mrs June Hall
Mrs Barbara Hardaker
Mr Robert Harrold
Tony Harrowsmith
Mrs Pauline Hasted
Dorothy and David Havenhand
Mr G E Hepworth
Bob Hesk
Mrs J Hill
Mr G A Hulme
J P Jeffries
Kevin Kelsall
David Lancaster
Ken Lewis
Jackie Mann
Ronald Martin
Tara Meahan
Mrs Barbara Mills
John and Shirley Moorse
Terry Morgan
K N Myer
Joan Nance

Ian Neville
Mr J Noble
Roy Norcliffe
Mrs Susan Pace
Gary Peek
William Plews
Alan Pugh
Alan Reaney
Rosemary Roberts
Andrew Ross
David Sands
Mark Saxby
P Scott-Wade
John F Shipley
Hubert Simper
June Sinfield
Mr and Mrs B Smith
Jean Smith
Mr K K Smith
W D Snowden
Mr M Spedding
John Storey
John Sykes
Ken and Helen Tulloch
Mr J G Waddinton
Mrs W Williams
Bill Willis
Rev E C Willis
Peter Wilson
Pam Young